CONFRONTATION
Challenging Others to Change

JUNE HUNT

AspirePress

Confrontation: Challenging Others to Change

© 2013 Hope For The Heart

Published by Aspire Press
an imprint of Hendrickson Publishing Group
Rose Publishing, LLC
P.O. Box 3473
Peabody, Massachusetts 01961-3473
www.hendricksonpublishinggroup.com

ISBN 978-1-59636-688-6

For more information on Hope For The Heart, visit www.hopefortheheart.org or call 1-800-488-HOPE (4673).

*Printed in the United States of America
January 2021, 5th printing*

CONTENTS

ear friend,

Confrontation has never been comfortable for me. At times I've felt that I would rather have the "black plague" than to have to confront someone. However, over the years I have moved from reluctance to the realization that confrontation with the right spirit—to expose the wrong and establish the right—is a biblical mandate. Confrontation is intended to establish truth for the purpose of conviction, correction, and a changed life. Galatians 6:1 tells us, *"If someone is caught in a sin, you who are spiritual should restore him gently."*

In the early days of our ministry at HOPE FOR THE HEART, I didn't want to confront "Blake," a fellow staff member—but knew I had to. Blake was a bright, creative, meticulous young man—and quick-tempered. He would become enraged over problems like a jammed copier and then he would take his wrath out on certain staff members. Unfortunately, his verbal abuse began to affect the spirit and morale of others.

After requesting a meeting with Blake, I applied the "sandwich technique"—two soft slices of bread with the meat of the matter in the middle.

The top slice of "bread" was appreciation: expressing my care and concern for Blake, sincerely complimenting him on the positives he brought to our ministry.

"Blake, you know that I genuinely care about you, don't you?"

He responded, "Yes, I do." I was grateful for that.

Then I moved to the meat of concern: confrontation. "Blake, whatever we do at Hope For The Heart has to be internally true to our name. We have to give hope to our own family inside our ministry, not just to those outside our ministry."

Now I had to address Blake's angry behavior: "Blake, the way you treat other team members is a problem. Your actions don't give them hope for their hearts. You are not helping them, but hurting them. It's just not working."

I reminded him how Jesus never placed projects as a higher priority than people. Then I shared my view of givers versus takers. "Blake, I want to say this to help you in the future. In life there are two kinds of people: givers and takers. Unfortunately, at this time in your life, I see you as a taker. I want you to go before God and ask if this is true. Realize, the Bible says, *'It is more blessed to give than to receive.'* Blake, I want you to be a giver. Throughout life, I want you to ask, 'What can I give to others' rather than 'What can I get from others?'"

Blake's pensive spirit indicated that he was absorbing every word of my concern. Now it was time to move to the bottom piece of "bread" in the sandwich: exhortation. I told Blake I believed in him. I knew he could be an encourager of others. I knew he could be a giver. I knew he could become the man God created him to be.

Not too long afterward, Blake took another position in Europe, and a year later when he returned to Dallas for a visit, he asked for time to meet with me.

Within the first three minutes of our conversation Blake said, "June, you were exactly right. I see now I was a taker and not a giver. Because of what you said, I saw where I needed to change—and I became determined to change. Thank you so much for telling me the truth. I had never seen this about myself until you confronted me."

Confrontation: Expose what's wrong—then establish what is right. My prayer is that you will have the courage to confront others when prompted by God to do so. I also pray that because of your Christ-like spirit, others—like Blake—may experience conviction, correction, and a truly changed life.

Yours in the Lord's hope,

June Hunt

P.S. This verse says it perfectly: *"Let your conversation be always full of grace, seasoned with salt, so that you may know how to answer everyone"* (Colossians 4:6).

CONFRONTATION
Challenging Others to Change

"Adam, Eve, where are you?" The probing voice of God pierces the evening air, confronting the two pounding hearts hiding in the foliage. Just hours before, all was so perfect, so peaceful, but when they ate the forbidden fruit, everything changed. They chose to disobey God—they chose to defy His authority—and now they flinch in fear as they hear His voice come nearer and nearer.

As they step out of their hiding, how will God confront the guilty couple? Things could have been so different. He created this first man and first woman and placed them in a perfect environment where He planned to meet all of their needs. If only they had listened to Him! If only they had trusted Him! If only they had obeyed Him! But, because of their fatal choice, they forfeited His perfect plan. Now what will He say to them, and what will be His approach? How will He confront their sin?

For the first time, rather than being at peace with God, the couple cowers in fear at His presence. God responds with questions: *"Who told you that you were naked? Have you eaten from the tree that I commanded you not to eat from?"*

God turns and asks Eve, *"What is this you have done?"* Although God clearly knew all that had transpired in their lives that day, He chose to confront both of them with questions—questions to expose their sin and establish the truth—to expose wrong in order to establish right (Genesis 3:9, 11, 13).

DEFINITIONS CONCERNING CONFRONTATION

Like Adam and Eve, most of us do not like having our sin exposed. Like them, we try to cover it up—to hide all evidence—in an effort to not "get caught." Basically, we do whatever we possibly can to avoid having to face the consequences of our bad choices. Our preference is to figure out a way to "get away with it" to somehow "make it go away" or, at the very least, not to have to "take responsibility for it." Assuming this behavior is natural and common to all humans, how do we deal with wrongdoing? How do we face our own "demons," and how do we handle the demons of others?

Clearly, the answer is not by ignoring, avoiding, hiding, or covering up offenses. But what is the answer? If we use the way God dealt with Adam and Eve as our model, then we must acknowledge bad behavior, face the consequences of bad behavior, and make efforts to change bad behavior. We must expose what is wrong to establish what is right. That process is called "confrontation," and it requires wisdom and discernment.

"Wisdom is found on the lips of the discerning, but a rod is for the back of him who lacks judgment."
(Proverbs 10:13)

▶ *Confrontation* is encountering a person in order to expose what is wrong, with the goal of establishing truth; confronting what is wrong to establish what is right.[1]

▶ *Confronting* a person helps establish the truth for the purpose of conviction, correction, and a change of life.

- The Hebrew word *tokhot* means "to correct, rebuke."[2] Solomon, the wisest man, understood the value of confrontation when he wrote, *"The corrections of discipline are the way to life"* (Proverbs 6:23).

- At times God will guide you to confront so that others can see their need to change as well as know what and how to change.

**"The grace of God. ...
It teaches us to say 'No' to ungodliness
and worldly passions, and to live
self-controlled, upright and godly lives
in this present age. ... These, then,
are the things you should teach.
Encourage and *rebuke*
with all authority."
(Titus 2:11–12, 15)**

Most people are fairly opinionated about how God confronts mortal human beings in the Bible. Typically, people picture God as pointing a bony finger while pounding a gavel in severe judgment upon some puny human—but this is not so.

As our loving God created the human race with immense diversity, He also uses various and diverse methods to confront according to each individual's need. From questions asked of Adam and Eve in Genesis to His rebuke of the churches in Revelation, undeniably God uses various methods of confrontation.

The same can be said of God's anointed people. There are many examples in Scripture of God using His people to confront ungodliness through a variety of methods in both the Old and the New Testaments. Each method, whether direct or indirect, is used with the loving intent of confronting what is wrong and establishing what is right so that we will become all He created us to be. Such confrontations require a response.

**"My son, do not despise
the LORD's discipline
and do not resent his rebuke,
because the LORD disciplines those he loves,
as a father the son he delights in."
(Proverbs 3:11–12)**

Method #1

Confronting with a Question (Indirect)
Job chapter 38:1–42:6

Have you witnessed the wisdom of those who ask many questions of others though they already know the answers? These intuitive individuals have discovered a powerful secret: Asking wise questions helps others gain insight into truth through inner reflection. In the Bible, Job begins reflecting on his wrong thinking, *knowing* that God will confront him.

**"What will I do when God confronts me?
What will I answer when called to account?"
(Job 31:14)**

▶ **The purpose of wise questioning** is to get people to think seriously about their attitudes and actions, to rethink their thoughts and reconsider their conclusions, to acknowledge their actions and examine their intentions. This method of confrontation is less about a question to evoke an answer and more about a challenge to evoke a change.

▶ **The power of wise questioning** is used by the Lord God Almighty.

In all literature, the most dramatic example of wise questioning is found in the book of Job. Job begins to doubt God's goodness. In turn, God begins His inquisition of Job with this question, *"Who is this that darkens my counsel with words without knowledge? Brace yourself like a man; I will question you, and you shall answer me"* (Job 38:2–3).

- Pertinent questions can be powerful. Through one question after another—literally 72 questions—God reveals His very nature to Job.

- Pertinent questions can be convicting. After hearing God's questions, Job is so deeply moved with conviction that he says, *"I despise myself and repent in dust and ashes"* (Job 42:6).

▶ **The skill of wise questioning** is used by wise counselors.

If you are one who understands and uses this technique, you have learned an essential counseling skill. God, our ultimate Counselor, demonstrates throughout Scripture that questions effectively draw others out to think about themselves and to think for themselves.

Some questions that appeal to the conscience are:

- "Do you want to live your life with true contentment?"

- "Do you want to be a person of total integrity?"

- "Do you want to fulfill God's purpose for your life?"

- "Do you want to have God's blessing on your life?"

"The purposes of a man's heart are deep waters, but a man of understanding draws them out." (Proverbs 20:5)

Method #2

Confronting with a Parable (Indirect)
Luke 20:9–19

Parables have long been recognized as food for thought and refreshing nourishment for the soul. Simple parables appeal to people of all ages—young and old alike. No wonder these memorable allegories have passed the test of time to remain classic lessons through the centuries.

▶ A **parable** is a short, fictitious illustration—a parable in Scripture is an earthly story with a heavenly meaning—focusing on one moral or spiritual truth.

▶ The Greek word *parabole* means comparison or illustration.[3] The parable, when used in Scripture, illustrates a moral or spiritual truth by using simple, everyday objects and settings.

▶ A parable shines a probing light on the darkness within our hearts and challenges us to change. Parables can have unending value in developing godly character in our lives.

A parable of a vineyard owner was used by Jesus to expose the dark motives within the hearts of Jewish leaders—the Scribes and Pharisees (Luke 20:9–19).

The owner of a vineyard rents out his land. At harvest time, the owner sends one servant after another to obtain some of the fruit; however, the tenants treat each servant shamefully. When the owner sends his beloved son, the tenants plot and kill him. Then Jesus said, *"What then will the owner of the vineyard do to them? He will come and kill those tenants and give the vineyard to others"* (Luke 20:15–16).

In telling this parable, Jesus established the truth—He knew the Scribes and Pharisees would plot to kill him. The tenants in the parable represent the Jewish leaders; the owner's servants represent the prophets of God whom Israel had murdered throughout the ages; and the owner's son represents Jesus.

In using this parable, Jesus confronted the Jewish leaders' abuse of the oversight God had entrusted to them. Rather than allowing the truth within the parable to convict them and seeing it as an opportunity to correct their wrong ways, they sought to kill Jesus.

> *"The teachers of the law and the chief priests looked for a way to arrest him immediately, because they knew he had spoken this parable against them. But they were afraid of the people."* (Luke 20:19)

Method #3

Confronting with a True-to-Life Story (Indirect) 2 Samuel 12:1–13

A story, if told well, has the power to move our emotions to anger or move our hearts to tears. Everyone responds to a well-told, true-to-life story. When people are blind to the truth of their own sin, telling them a story parallel to their own sin can be powerfully convicting.

The true story of David's adulterous affair is recorded in the Bible. David, in his amorous pursuit of Bathsheba, impregnated her and then murdered her husband and married her to cover up his sinful actions. Because of David's position as king, he escaped the legal consequences of his crimes—the consequences he would have brought on his subjects if they had committed such acts.

▶ **A true-to-life story can have a spiritual purpose.** The Lord sent Nathan to confront David through a skillfully told story about two men. One was rich, and the other was poor. The rich man had many flocks of sheep, but the poor man had only one beloved pet lamb. When preparing a meal for a traveler, the rich man refused to pick a sheep from his own large flock and instead took the poor man's little lamb to serve to his guest. After Nathan told this story, David passed the most severe judgment on this rich man.

"David burned with anger against the man and said to Nathan, 'As surely as the LORD lives, the man who did this deserves to die!'" (2 Samuel 12:5)

▶ **A true-to-life story can be powerful.** David's instant judgment against the rich man was absolutely justified. So what could he say when Nathan turned the tables on him saying, *"You are the man!"* (2 Samuel 12:7)?

▶ **A true-to-life story can be convicting.** In listening, David realized how his lust had led to adultery, his adultery to deceit, and his deceit to murder. As a result of this confrontation, he repented and said, *"I have sinned against the LORD"* (2 Samuel 12:13).

▶ **A true-to-life story can cause a change of life.** Convicting stories can serve to create a hunger to have a pure heart before God. Following David's moral failure with Bathsheba and Nathan's subsequent confrontation, he said, *"Create in me a pure heart, O God, and renew a steadfast spirit within me"* (Psalm 51:10).

Method #4

Confronting with an Admonition (Direct)
John 8:1–11

We are all created with a conscience by which we gauge whether an attitude or action is *right* or *wrong*. Christians also have the convicting work of the Holy Spirit within their hearts. Feeling guilt is appropriate when we stray from the truth and engage in wrongful acts—this is "true guilt." If we stay in sin for a long time without responding to appropriate guilt, we can develop a "seared conscience." At times, however, God appeals to our conscience by sending some individual to confront us.

▶ An **admonition** is a gentle confrontation of warning or counsel for the purpose of correction. To admonish in a gentle, earnest manner means to warn or counsel a person who is in the wrong.

  ▪ The Greek word *noutheteo* means to "admonish" or literally "to put in mind" (*nous* = mind, *tithemi* = to put).[4]

▶ An admonition is an earnest, friendly warning given in order to train a person's mind to think and therefore to act differently.

The apostle Paul said, *"Let the word of Christ dwell in you richly as you teach and admonish one another with all wisdom, and as you sing psalms, hymns and spiritual songs with gratitude in your hearts to God"* (Colossians 3:16).

One day, a woman is caught in the act of adultery. The religious leaders bring her before Jesus, wanting Him to pronounce the death sentence by stoning. Instead of confronting the woman, Jesus confronts the judgmental attitudes of the Scribes and Pharisees by appealing to their conscience.

Jesus cleverly turns the tables on these accusers by highlighting their focus on the letter of the law and their obvious lack of grace. Because they are looking at the letter of the law, Jesus challenges them to first judge themselves in light of the law.

▶ **An admonition can convict a person's conscience.** Jesus' confrontation appeals to their conscience. Jesus makes them look first at their own actions: *"He who is without sin among you, let him throw a stone at her first"* (John 8:7 NKJV). No one moves—eventually being convicted by their own conscience, they all depart one by one, leaving only Jesus and the woman standing alone.

▶ **An admonition can encourage a change of life.** Now, for the first time, Jesus addresses the woman and her wrongful actions.

"When Jesus had raised Himself up and saw no one but the woman, He said to her, 'Woman, where are those accusers of yours? Has no one condemned you?' She said, 'No one, Lord.' And Jesus said to her,

'Neither do I condemn you; go and sin no more.'"
(John 8:10–11 NKJV)

When you are confronting one caught in sin, examples of some ways to appeal to the conscience are to use comments like these:

- "You can gain and maintain a clear conscience. I want to help you."

- "You can be free of any temptation and not be continually hooked."

- "You can have the blessing of God on your life. I want that for you. Is that what you want?"

Method #5

Confronting with a Rebuke (Direct)
Matthew 16:21–23

At times, the most appropriate way to confront is to be direct and explicit, for instance when someone does something flagrantly wrong or when a bad role model corrupts a child's conscience. Directly exposing someone when they offend does risk alienating them, but at times this method is necessary to turn hearts and to correct a negative situation.

▶ A **rebuke** is a stern, strict reprimand or a convincing, convicting reproof used in order to correct a fault. To rebuke is to confront those in the wrong directly with the aim of *charging* or *challenging* them to do what is right.

- The Greek word *epitimao* is translated "rebuke."[5] During the crucifixion of Christ, one repentant thief rebuked the other thief—he *challenged* him to change: *"The other criminal rebuked him. 'Don't you fear God,' he said, 'since you are under the same sentence?'"* (Luke 23:40).

▶ To rebuke can also mean to confront those in the wrong with the aim of **convincing** or **convicting** them to do right.

- The Greek word *elegcho*, which is often translated "rebuke," also means "to convict, convince or reprove."[6]

  "You have forgotten that word of encouragement that addresses you as sons: 'My son, do not make light of the Lord's discipline, and do not lose heart when he rebukes you.'" (Hebrews 12:5)

▶ A **double rebuke** occurred after Jesus told His followers that He must be killed and three days later rise again. Not grasping God's plan, Peter rebuked Jesus and, in turn, Jesus rebuked Peter.

"Peter took him aside and began to rebuke him. 'Never, Lord!' he said. 'This shall never happen to you!'" (Matthew 16:22)

There is no more powerful rebuke than the one from Jesus to Peter: *"When Jesus turned and looked at his disciples, he rebuked Peter. 'Get behind me, Satan!' he said. 'You do not have in mind the things of God, but the things of men'"* (Mark 8:33).

▶ A **correct rebuke** requires that the direct confrontation be balanced with great patience and careful instruction in order to bring about change.

"Correct, rebuke and encourage—with great patience and careful instruction." (2 Timothy 4:2)

WHAT IS God's Heart on Confrontation?

The goal of confrontation is not to point a pious finger at someone else's sin, but to point to the truth that correction is necessary—the kind of truth that sets us free, turns us around, and puts us on a correction course.

Have you ever unknowingly been walking the wrong way? How you wished for someone who cared enough to intervene, to challenge you, to confront you. You needed to be put on a "correction course."

At times we all need to be confronted with truth, an act that can result in *conviction*, *correction*, and a *change of direction*. Confrontation, if done wisely and if wisely heeded, is often used by God to correct us from going the wrong way and to cause us to start going the right way.

> **"The way of a fool seems right to him,
> but a wise man listens to advice."
> (Proverbs 12:15)**

▶ The Purpose of Positive Confrontation

The Spirit of God confronts sin in the life of a nonbeliever in order to bring that person to confession, repentance, and salvation. Likewise, the Spirit of God confronts sin in the life of a Christian in order to produce confession, repentance, and Christlikeness.

Jesus died not just to save you from the penalty of sin (eternal separation from God), but also to save you from the power of sin in your life. Therefore, sin must be confronted so that you can be set free from its bondage. At times, confrontation is necessary both for salvation and for victorious living.

Based on God's love ...

- God confronts us in order to keep us walking within His will and in close relationship with Him.

  "Know then in your heart that as a man disciplines his son, so the LORD your God disciplines you. Observe the commands of the Lord your God, walking in his ways and revering him." (Deuteronomy 8:5–6)

- God gives us the task of wise confrontation to help others see their need to have a personal relationship with Christ or to become more Christlike.

  "We proclaim him, admonishing and teaching everyone with all wisdom, so that we may present everyone perfect in Christ." (Colossians 1:28)

- God confronts us because He loves us as a father loves his child. He wants to make us holy, as He is holy, so that we can live at peace with others.

"Our fathers disciplined us for a little while as they thought best; but God disciplines us for our good, that we may share in his holiness. No discipline seems pleasant at the time, but painful. Later on, however, it produces a harvest of righteousness and peace for those who have been trained by it." (Hebrews 12:10–11)

- God confronts us by using His Word to equip us for life.

"All Scripture is God-breathed and is useful for teaching, rebuking, correcting and training in righteousness, so that the man of God may be thoroughly equipped for every good work." (2 Timothy 3:16–17)

▶ **The Peril of Negative Confrontation**

Confrontation that should be helpful and healing can miss the mark by becoming *harmful* and *hostile* when the motive is self-centered and the method is self-serving.

- *Harmful Confrontation*

Righteous Job lamented that his friends were wrong to confront him in the midst of his intense suffering. After they confronted him, he cried out to them, *"Miserable comforters are you all! ... I also could speak like you, if you were in my place; I could make fine speeches against you and shake my head at you. But my mouth would encourage you; comfort from my lips would bring you relief"* (Job 16:2–5).

▪ Hostile Confrontation

David, too, wrote about how the Lord delivered him from the hostile confrontation of his enemies and specifically from the hand of King Saul: *"The cords of the grave coiled around me; the snares of death confronted me. ... He rescued me from my powerful enemy, from my foes, who were too strong for me. They confronted me in the day of my disaster, but the LORD was my support"* (2 Samuel 22:6, 18–19).

WHAT ARE the Four Styles of Confrontation?

Does the thought of confronting someone make you want to run for cover? Awkward situations that call for confrontation can cause great emotional strain—even ruining a close relationship. Have you tiptoed around a problem, hoping it will go away? Or have you stuffed your anger only to have it build and later erupt like a volcano in the face of your offender? Ultimately, we need to overcome our fear and have the courage to lovingly confront by living in the light of God's truth.

**"The LORD is my light and my salvation—
whom shall I fear?
The LORD is the stronghold of my life—
of whom shall I be afraid?"
(Psalm 27:1)**

David's life illustrates four distinct styles of dealing with difficult people.

#1 The Passive Style: The *Avoider* confronts indirectly by using silence or nonspecific language to communicate needs and desires.

▶ Shuns direct interaction because of fear

▶ Expects others to figure out what is wanted

GOAL: Avoiding confrontation to ensure self-protection

DISADVANTAGES: Produces no long-term solution and leads to bigger problems

EXAMPLE: At one time David chose to be *silent* and to avoid saying anything at all around his offenders; however, his passive approach only increased the anguish and anger within his heart.

"I [David] said, 'I will watch my ways and keep my tongue from sin; I will put a muzzle on my mouth as long as the wicked are in my presence.' But when I was silent and still, not even saying anything good, my anguish increased. My heart grew hot within me, and as I meditated, the fire burned; then I spoke with my tongue." (Psalm 39:1–3)

#2 The Aggressive Style: The *Attacker* confronts by overtly attacking the character of the other person in order to gain power.

▶ Uses threats and intimidation to get needs met by others at any cost

▶ Feels free to violate the rights of others

GOAL: Gaining power and control through anger or force

DISADVANTAGES: Produces only short-term solutions and makes enemies by hurting feelings

EXAMPLE: Many of David's enemies levied all-out *attacks* in order to bring David down.

"My slanderers pursue me all day long; many are attacking me in their pride." (Psalm 56:2)

#3 The Passive-Aggressive Style: The *Ambusher* confronts by covertly ambushing the other person as a power play.

▶ Uses sarcasm and sniping rather than direct, specific language

▶ Tries to get even at a later time for real or imagined slights

GOAL: Avoiding direct responses and accountability while "getting even"

DISADVANTAGES: Produces no solutions and expresses destructive anger in indirect ways

EXAMPLE: Repeatedly, David was verbally *ambushed* with indirect attacks from his passive-aggressive offenders.

"Hide me from the conspiracy of the wicked. ... They sharpen their tongues like swords and aim their words like deadly arrows. They shoot from ambush at the innocent man." (Psalm 64:2–4)

#4 The Assertive Style: The *Activator* confronts by directly affirming the truth that positive change needs to take place.

▶ Uses direct, specific language to express factual information

▶ Confronts directly in a way that expresses value for the opinions and feelings of others

GOAL: Presenting the facts, correcting untruths, and changing behavior

ADVANTAGES: Produces effective solutions and builds long-term trust and respect

EXAMPLE: On two different occasions David had the opportunity to put to death his enemy King Saul, but rather than act aggressively, he chose to spare Saul's life and confront him assertively.

"Why do you listen when men say, 'David is bent on harming you'? This day you have seen with your own eyes how the LORD delivered you into my hands in the cave. Some urged me to kill you, but I spared you; I said, 'I will not lift my hand against my master, because he is the LORD's anointed.' ... May the LORD judge between you and me. ... And may the LORD avenge the wrongs you have done to me, but my hand will not touch you." (1 Samuel 24:9–10, 12)

CHARACTERISTICS OF CONFRONTATION

Do you confront when you shouldn't—and do you avoid confronting when you should? A strong religious leader confronts a woman when she is acting drunk in church, but she is actually in anguish, crying out to God because she can't conceive a child. That leader aggressively confronts her based only on appearances and before he knows the facts. (See 1 Samuel 1:9–18.)

This same leader who confronts when he shouldn't is later guilty of *not* confronting when he *should*. He fails to confront his two contemptible sons when they abuse their position as priests and take advantage of God's people. (See 1 Samuel 2:12–36.) God rebukes Eli for his *passivity* because he fails to protect the people.

Fear of conflict can make you passively do nothing or misunderstanding can cause you to confront inappropriately. Knowing when and how to confront requires wisdom.

In his old age, Eli finally confronts his sons—but by then it's too late. Eli pays a high price for being too passive. God tells Eli that He will ...

**"Judge his family forever because
of the sin he knew about;
his sons made themselves contemptible,
and he failed to restrain them."
(1 Samuel 3:13)**

Since there is a wrong time to confront when it does more damage than good and a right time to confront when it serves God's purpose, how do you know when the time is right?

You Should Confront ...

▶ **When someone is in danger.** Some people say or do things that hurt themselves or others to the extent that lives are at risk. God opposes all abusive behavior, whether it is self-inflicted or inflicted onto others. You need to intervene when you see any behavior that puts people in harm's way.

"Rescue those being led away to death; hold back those staggering toward slaughter. If you say, 'But we knew nothing about this,' does not he who weighs the heart perceive it? Does not he who guards your life know it? Will he not repay each person according to what he has done?" (Proverbs 24:11–12)

▶ **When a relationship is threatened.**
Relationships are vulnerable to damaging words or actions. You need to confront when necessary to preserve the relationship.

"I plead with Euodia and I plead with Syntyche to agree with each other in the Lord. Yes, and I ask you, loyal yokefellow, help these women who have contended at my side in the cause of the gospel, along with Clement and the rest of my fellow workers, whose names are in the book of life." (Philippians 4:2–3)

▶ **When division exists within a group.** One of the enemy's tactics is to cause quarrels, strife, and jealousy among a body of believers. God calls us to unity, agreement, and peace. He charges us to guard and protect these precious relationships.

"Let us therefore make every effort to do what leads to peace and to mutual edification." (Romans 14:19)

▶ **When someone sins against you.** Difficult though it may be, God gives you a clear directive to confront anyone who does something to you that clearly violates God's will in regard to how you are to be treated.

"If your brother sins against you, go and show him his fault, just between the two of you. If he listens to you, you have won your brother over." (Matthew 18:15)

▶ **When you are offended.** Sometimes you can be offended by someone's actions even when the actions are not sinful. For the sake of the relationship, confronting in humility and exposing your concern allows the other person to be sensitive to you in the future and to not intentionally offend you by continuing the offensive actions.

"Be completely humble and gentle; be patient, bearing with one another in love. Make every effort to keep the unity of the Spirit through the bond of peace." (Ephesians 4:2–3)

▶ **When someone is caught in a sin.** At times you will see a sin in others to which they are blind. While guarding against the possibility of the same sin in your own life, God wants to use you to expose the sin and help the one trapped to overcome it.

"When I [God] say to a wicked man, 'You will surely die,' and you do not warn him or speak out to dissuade him from his evil ways in order to save his life, that wicked man will die for his sin, and I will hold you accountable for his blood." (Ezekiel 3:18)

▶ **When others are offended.** Sometimes confronting on behalf of others is appropriate. In cases of prejudice, injustice, or violence toward those unable to defend themselves, God expects you to take up their cause and speak out against the wrong done to them. The apostle Paul confronted Peter openly,

"I opposed him to his face, because he was clearly in the wrong. Before certain men came from James, he used to eat with the Gentiles. But when they [the Jews] arrived, he began to draw back and separate himself from the Gentiles because he was afraid of those who belonged to the circumcision group. The other Jews joined him in his hypocrisy, so that by their hypocrisy even Barnabas was led astray." (Galatians 2:11–13)

QUESTION: "Why can't I just forgive and forget? Why do I have to confront someone when they offend me?"

ANSWER: Undisclosed forgiveness benefits you by keeping you from becoming bitter, but it does not necessarily benefit your offender who is in need of correction. Yes, you need to forgive and not dwell on the offense, but you also need to confront in order to make your offender aware of a problem area that needs to be addressed. Forgiving without confronting can later result in your offender's resenting you for not caring enough to make the offense known so that the bad behavior could be changed. Your offender could then develop a bitter root that later bears bitter fruit.[8]

> "See to it that no one misses the grace of God and that no bitter root grows up to cause trouble and defile many."
> (Hebrews 12:15)

WHEN SHOULD You Not Confront?[9]

While confrontation can create unity, it can also divide. To avoid needless damage, you should not confront ...

▶ **When you are not the right person to confront.** If you are not the one offended or not responsible for the one offended, you may not be the one who should confront. However, God might use you to help the person who is responsible to confront.

"Like one who seizes a dog by the ears is a passer-by who meddles in a quarrel not his own." (Proverbs 26:17)

▶ **When it's not the right time to confront.** You may be the right person to do the confronting, but it may not be the right time or your heart may not be right.

"There is a time for everything ... a time to be silent and a time to speak." (Ecclesiastes 3:1, 7)

▶ **When you are uncertain of the facts.** Be sure you are fully informed of what is happening. Sometimes asking the right questions and listening objectively will reveal that you are simply misperceiving the situation.

"He who answers before listening—that is his folly and his shame." (Proverbs 18:13)

▶ **When it's best to overlook a minor offense.** You may find that overlooking minor offenses allows God to convict others of their errors. When in doubt, erring on the side of restraint and mercy is generally best.

"Hatred stirs up dissension, but love covers over all wrongs." (Proverbs 10:12)

▶ **When you are committing the same sin.** Paradoxically, you can be most offended by people who are engaging in the very behaviors with which you yourself struggle. We are hypocritical if we try to correct others when we ourselves are guilty of the same thing. First correct your own behavior. Then you can help correct the behavior of someone else.

"Why do you look at the speck of sawdust in your brother's eye and pay no attention to the plank in your own eye? How can you say to your brother, 'Let me take the speck out of your eye,' when all the time there is a plank in your own eye? You hypocrite, first take the plank out of your own eye, and then you will see clearly to remove the speck from your brother's eye." (Matthew 7:3–5)

▶ **When your motive is purely your own rights, not the benefit of the other person.** A "my rights" attitude will only damage the spirit of a positive confrontation. Therefore, consider another's interests over your own.

"Do nothing out of selfish ambition or vain conceit, but in humility consider others better than yourselves. Each of you should look not only to your own interests, but also to the interests of others." (Philippians 2:3–4)

▶ **When you have a vindictive motive.** Before you confront, genuine forgiveness of the offender is imperative. In your heart, release the offender into the hands of God. Your confrontation must not be to satisfy your secret desire to take revenge or to get even.

"Do not repay anyone evil for evil. Be careful to do what is right in the eyes of everybody." (Romans 12:17)

▶ **When the consequences of the confrontation outweigh those of the offense.** Look at the degree of the offense before you confront. Some battles pay little dividends and are just not worth the fight!

"Better a dry crust with peace and quiet than a house full of feasting, with strife." (Proverbs 17:1)

▶ **When the person you want to confront has a habit of foolishness and quarreling.** Avoid confronting people who are unwilling to recognize their offense. If you cannot avoid the confrontation, you may need to take others with you to help in confronting these persons.

"Don't have anything to do with foolish and stupid arguments, because you know they produce quarrels. And the Lord's servant must not quarrel; instead, he must be kind to everyone, able to teach, not resentful." (2 Timothy 2:23–24)

▶ **When setting aside your rights will benefit an unbeliever.** Jesus modeled suffering for righteousness' sake and exhorts you to endure unjust hardship for the sake of exposing God's character to the unbeliever. Allow room for God to work in another's heart by showing restraint.

"It is commendable if a man bears up under the pain of unjust suffering because he is conscious of God. ... To this you were called, because Christ suffered for you, leaving you an example, that you should follow in his steps." (1 Peter 2:19, 21)

▶ **When the person who offended you is your enemy.** Sometimes it is best not to confront but to win them over by praying for them and blessing them. You and your offender are ultimately responsible to God for your actions. The path to peace might mean forgiving and blessing your offender without ever confronting the offensive behavior.

"Love your enemies and pray for those who persecute you, that you may be sons of your Father in heaven. He causes his sun to rise on the evil and the good, and sends rain on the righteous and the unrighteous." (Matthew 5:44–45)

▶ **When confrontation will be ineffective and reprisal severe.** You may not be able to effectively confront a person who has a violent temper and who is likely to exact severe retribution on you or on someone you love. (However, with such a person you still need to have and enforce proper boundaries.)

"Whoever corrects a mocker invites insult; whoever rebukes a wicked man incurs abuse." (Proverbs 9:7)

QUESTION: "If I have a Christian friend who is continuing to live in sin, am I obligated to confront my friend?"

ANSWER: Realize that you may be God's agent to help your friend change and then grow to be more Christlike. If you care enough to confront, God can use you to encourage and support different loved ones to overcome habits that enslave them or alienate them from others. At times He will call you to directly but lovingly intervene in the lives of fellow believers who have wandered from the truth and have become ensnared by sin.

"My brothers, if one of you should wander from the truth and someone should bring him back, remember this: Whoever turns a sinner from the error of his way will save him from death and cover over a multitude of sins." (James 5:19–20)

If you are involved in a conflict requiring confrontation and you realize you need to confront, be aware that you may make the mistake of using one of three negative strategies: *avoiding, attacking,* or *ambushing.*

▶ If you are *Passive/Avoider ...*

- Your strategy is to completely avoid the problem without ever addressing the person directly.

- You have a fear-based mentality, perhaps learned in childhood, that could make you feel unworthy or inadequate to confront.

- You are overly compliant wanting to avoid disagreement, and you cower out of fear.

- By avoiding confrontation, however, you allow the sinful behavior of the other person to continue creating relational conflicts.

The Bible records King Saul's confession: *"I have sinned. ... I was afraid of the people and so I gave in to them"* (1 Samuel 15:24).

▶ If you are *Aggressive/Attacker ...*

- Your strategy is to attack the other person, not the problem.

- You build up your own self-esteem by attacking and suppressing others.

- You feel entitled to cross the personal boundaries of another person's space, work, time, or personal life. You seek to control others by intimidation.

- By attacking, you may win the momentary battle, but you lose the ultimate war. Your inappropriate attacks harm the relationship and provide no lasting resolution for correcting offensive behavior.

The Bible says, *"The LORD detests all the proud of heart. Be sure of this: They will not go unpunished"* (Proverbs 16:5).

▶ If you are *Passive–Aggressive/Ambusher* ...

- Your strategy is to ambush the other person without confronting the problem.

- You are afraid and prefer hiding, manipulating, and ambushing in order to gain power rather than directly confronting.

- You keep a record of real or imagined offenses to justify getting even. You find it difficult to accept responsibility for hurting others, and you act as a "sniper," shooting slander, sarcasm, and mocking remarks from a distance.

- By ambushing, you avoid a direct confrontation while at the same time you look for subtle ways to make a power play. Your relational conflicts are never resolved because you never deal with them.

The Bible says, *"A mocker resents correction; he will not consult the wise"* (Proverbs 15:12).

▶ If you are ***Assertive/Activater*** (a positive strategy!) ...

- Your strategy is to actively assert yourself by confronting in order to resolve the problem.

- You deal fairly and respectfully with everyone involved by listening carefully, stating the truth, correcting untruth directly, and exposing areas where people differ or misunderstand one another.

- You make requests, taking the needs of others into account by courageously giving words of admonishment, rebuke, or encouragement when appropriate.

- By asserting yourself, you provide the greatest opportunity to have positive relationships because you speak with discernment and confidently confront with sound judgment.

"My son, preserve sound judgment and discernment, do not let them out of your sight. ... For the LORD *will be your confidence and will keep your foot from being snared."* (Proverbs 3:21, 26)

Certain other strategies may seem right for the moment, but they will not bring about godly results and will ultimately fail. Only an assertive strategy based on truth will succeed and stand the test of time.

The Bible says about those who have subversive strategies, *"Devise your strategy, but it will be thwarted; propose your plan, but it will not stand, for God is with us"* (Isaiah 8:10).

Deciding that you need to confront is one thing. Deciding what you need to say is another! Preparing your wording in advance will help you speak clearly and lovingly when the occasion for confrontation arises.

> **"A word aptly spoken**
> **is like apples of gold in settings of silver.**
> **Like an earring of gold or an ornament of**
> **fine gold is a wise man's rebuke**
> **to a listening ear."**
> **(Proverbs 25:11–12)**

▶ **Confronting unjust treatment on behalf of a coworker**

- "Maybe you felt he was not doing his job adequately, but do you think it is fair to fire him without allowing him an opportunity to change?"

- "You might encourage him by pointing out the improvements that need to take place within his area of responsibility."

▶ **Confronting a friend who is excessively late**

- "I thought we were to meet for lunch at 1:00. I have been waiting here for an hour. Did I misunderstand the time we agreed on?"

▶ Confronting a friend who violates your personal boundaries

- "Please know that I enjoy talking with you, but we need to talk at earlier times in the evening. I really need to get more sleep at night; therefore, let's not call each other past 9:00 p.m."

▶ Confronting a spouse for repeated failure to call when late for dinner

- "I've had dinner ready at 6:30 for the last five days, yet you've not called to say that you would be late. I need you to call me by 6:15 if you are not going to be on time. If you have not called by 6:30, the children and I will go ahead and eat."

▶ Confronting a coworker for gossip and slander

- "Would you tell me what you said to others about the project I've just finished?"

- "I heard that you actually said that you don't respect my work."

- "It would be helpful if you would come directly to me with your concerns. I sincerely want to do my best, and I will value your comments."

▶ Confronting others to help them see their blind spots

- "I know you have experienced a deep sense of betrayal by your friend. Do you think it is wise to continue to trust him?"

- "Do you think it is wise to put all your emotional eggs in one basket and not develop some other meaningful relationships?"

▶ **Confronting to set or enforce boundaries**

- "I did not stop coming over without a reason. You heard your mother request that I no longer help you with homework because she didn't want you to be dependent on outside help. Please understand that I enjoy working with you, but I must honor her request."

- "I thought you said you were not going to eat any more sweets after 7:00 p.m. Do you still want me to hold you accountable for that?"

CAUSES FOR A LACK OF CONFRONTATION

Do you know someone who is arrogant, rude, cruel, but continues to get away with it? While you wish he would change, deeper still, you wish he would get what he deserves!

That is exactly why one man refused to deliver a life-changing message to people he considered "the enemy." They were arrogant and cruel. He didn't want to confront them because they just might change and then they wouldn't have to pay for their cruelty.

God tells Jonah to go and confront the rebellious people of Nineveh. If they don't repent, God will destroy them—but Jonah wants them to be destroyed, so he refuses to warn them. Instead he boards a boat and heads in the opposite direction. That's when God uses a big storm and a big fish to reveal a big mistake. Finally, Jonah obeys God and confronts the people—but when they all repent and receive God's mercy, is Jonah grateful and glad? No—he resents God's mercy and carries a grudge. He wants them wiped out—he wants revenge. He simply sits down and sulks.

Jonah has a **passive-aggressive** mind-set:

▶ He passively remains silent so that the people will not repent.

▶ He aggressively does everything possible to keep them from receiving God's mercy.

Jonah's mind-set needs a major overhaul—he needs a boatload of mercy. Jonah could receive the blessing of God if only he would offer the mercy of God—Jonah needed to hear the words of Jesus:

> **"Blessed are the merciful,**
> **for they will be shown mercy."**
> **(Matthew 5:7)**

WHY IS It Difficult to Confront?

Although the Bible says much about the benefits of confrontation, we frequently avoid confronting those who offend us. Why do we sidestep a one-on-one encounter when it could restore a strained relationship?

It Is Difficult to Confront When ...

▶ **You are a shy person.** Confrontation does indeed take boldness and strong faith in the Lord.

- However, take heart, God will always give you His strength to do what is right.

    "I can do everything through him who gives me strength." (Philippians 4:13)

▶ **You risk more damage to the relationship.** If the offender does not respond properly, there is legitimate danger that the relationship may be damaged.

- However, by confronting with the proper spirit and in the proper way, you can trust God to bring about His purposes through your confrontation.

"He who ignores discipline despises himself, but whoever heeds correction gains understanding." (Proverbs 15:32)

▶ **You may hurt someone's feelings.** Sometimes confrontation does inflict emotional pain, but your intervention may help a person avoid suffering severe consequences of persistent, harmful behavior. Honesty in a friendship is more valuable than excessive praise and flattery.

- However, it is better to hurt a little now for a short time than to hurt a lot throughout a lifetime.

  "He who rebukes a man will in the end gain more favor than he who has a flattering tongue." (Proverbs 28:23)

▶ **You could risk advancement or career opportunities.** If you confront a coworker or even a supervisor, you do risk earning a reputation as a "confrontational" or "contentious" person.

- However, if you confront in love and with a correct attitude, your offender is likely to see that you are not trying to hurt them, but trying to help them.

  "Let your conversation be always full of grace, seasoned with salt, so that you may know how to answer everyone." (Colossians 4:6)

▶ **You know that you have faults and don't want to appear hypocritical.** It is true—no one is perfect.

- However, if you wait until you are perfect before you try to help others with their imperfections, you will never confront the sin in anyone's life. The requirement for confrontation is not perfection, but is compassionate reaching out to others who are struggling in sin.

"He who conceals his sins does not prosper, but whoever confesses and renounces them finds mercy." (Proverbs 28:13)

▶ **You have never seen proper, biblical confrontation.** Angry arguments and inappropriate accusations were the patterns modeled for you as a child.

- However, don't allow negative examples from your past to dissuade you from learning and practicing biblical confrontation.

"Do not conform any longer to the pattern of this world, but be transformed by the renewing of your mind. Then you will be able to test and approve what God's will is—his good, pleasing and perfect will." (Romans 12:2)

Two goals must be kept in balance when confronting someone: On the one hand, you need to expose the negative behavior—on the other hand, you need to maintain a respectful relationship. Three of the four approaches yield poor results because they do not keep this balance. Only one approach addresses the behavior problem and, at the same time, preserves the relationship.[11]

> **"There is a way that seems right to a man, but in the end it leads to death."**
> **(Proverbs 14:12)**

▶ **The Passive Approach: "Running Away—Staying Away"**

If you *avoid* confrontation because of fear, you resign yourself to maintain the mind-set, *I lose, you win.*

Instead ...

- Face your offender and set boundaries for the relationship. This will give a greater opportunity for you to eventually earn respect.

- Be willing to give up the relationship, if the offense is serious or the offender dangerous, in order to protect yourself and potentially motivate the offender to change.

"Do not rebuke a mocker or he will hate you; rebuke a wise man and he will love you." (Proverbs 9:8)

▶ **The Aggressive Approach: "My Way or the Highway"**

If your confrontation turns into an ***attack*** because you must be on top, you assume the position *I win, you lose!*

Instead ...

- Look beyond the short-term argument to win a mutually caring long-term relationship, which is the goal of successful confrontation. Seek to understand the deeper needs of your offender that are represented by the wrong behavior.

- Look for healthy compromise to produce necessary behavioral change in order to preserve the relationship with your offender.

"Do not take revenge, my friends, but leave room for God's wrath, for it is written: 'It is mine to avenge; I will repay,' says the Lord." (Romans 12:19)

▶ **The Passive-Aggressive Approach: "Have It Your Way—but You'll Pay"**

If you ***ambush*** the character of another person because you feel powerless, your goal is *I lose, but you lose too!*

Instead ...

- Avoid the trap of undermining the character of another rather than confronting directly. The temptation to slander or gossip is a passive-aggressive approach that fails to resolve the offensive behavior.

- Retreat temporarily from your offender, if necessary, but don't let your need to collect your thoughts be a reason to avoid confronting directly.

"A wise son heeds his father's instruction, but a mocker does not listen to rebuke." (Proverbs 13:1)

▶ The Assertive Approach: "God's Way—the Best Way"

When you ***assertively*** confront because you care about the relationship, thereby offering hope for a change in behavior, your goal is a win-win solution—*We both win!*

Realize ...

- The reward of an assertive confrontation is greater trust and respect, which results in a deeper and more satisfying relationship. And confrontation is a means for greater unity in the body of Christ.

- Assertive confrontation may produce short-term conflict, but it is often the means for long-term gain. Relationships can be strengthened and people's lives can be changed when you learn to confront assertively.

"I appeal to you, brothers, in the name of our Lord Jesus Christ, that all of you agree with one another so that there may be no divisions among you and that you may be perfectly united in mind and thought." (1 Corinthians 1:10)

The Bible is a relational book. It reveals God's holy standard for the way we are to interact with one another. You, therefore, have scriptural support to confront when someone violates God's standard and steps over your moral, physical, or emotional boundaries—or those of another person.

The 11 Commandments of Confrontation

#1 God declares that you are to show respect and are to be treated with respect.

"Show proper respect to everyone." (1 Peter 2:17)

#2 God declares that you are to speak truthfully from your heart and that others are to speak truthfully to you.

"Each of you must put off falsehood and speak truthfully to his neighbor." (Ephesians 4:25)

#3 God declares that you are to listen to others and that others should listen to you.

"Everyone should be quick to listen, slow to speak and slow to become angry." (James 1:19)

#4 God declares that you are to express appropriate anger and to have anger appropriately expressed toward you.

"In your anger do not sin." (Ephesians 4:26)

#5 God declares that you are to give and to receive only justifiable rebukes.

"He who listens to a life-giving rebuke will be at home among the wise." (Proverbs 15:31)

#6 God declares that you are to value and to protect your conscience.

"I strive always to keep my conscience clear before God and man." (Acts 24:16)

#7 God declares that you are to say *no* without feeling guilty.

"Say 'No' to ungodliness and worldly passions." (Titus 2:12)

#8 God declares that you are to remove yourself from an abusive situation.

"Do not make friends with a hot-tempered man, do not associate with one easily angered." (Proverbs 22:24)

#9 God declares that you are to bring opposing parties together to determine what is the real truth.

"The first to present his case seems right, till another comes forward and questions him." (Proverbs 18:17)

#10 God declares that you are to seek emotional and spiritual support from others.

"Let us not give up meeting together ... but let us encourage one another." (Hebrews 10:25)

#11 God declares that you are to appeal to a higher authority when necessary.

"If the charges brought against me by these Jews are not true, no one has the right to hand me over to them. I appeal to Caesar!" (Acts 25:11)

We all have three God-given inner needs, the need for love, for significance, and for security.[12] We can be controlled by fear if we adopt the wrong assumption that confronting an offender means that our basic inner needs will not be met. If you are unwilling to confront, you are living with the wrong assumptions. The Lord promises to meet your needs.

> **"My God will meet all your needs**
> **according to his glorious riches**
> **in Christ Jesus."**
> **(Philippians 4:19)**

▶ **WRONG BELIEFS ABOUT CONFRONTING:**

- The *passive* person says: "If I confront others, the end result will be bad—I will hurt, they will hurt, and our relationship will be hurt. By avoiding confrontation I can protect my basic needs from being threatened. The only way that I can please those around me is to keep silent."

- The *aggressive* person says: "If I don't strongly confront others, the end result will be bad—I will lose, they will win, and my goals will not succeed. By strongly confronting, I can ensure that my basic needs are met. The only way I can reach my goals is to dominate others."

- The *passive-aggressive* person says: "If I confront, I could be rejected—if I don't confront, I could be belittled. By masking my discontent, I can still find ways to make my point without risking personal loss. The only way I can reach my goals is to avoid direct confrontation but covertly attack from a safe distance."

▶ Right Belief about Confronting:

- The *assertive* person says: "I will neither be afraid of nor exaggerate opportunities to confront. Knowing that I am deeply loved, eternally secure, and truly significant, I will be willing to confront with confidence, knowing that confrontation can produce positive growth and change."

"Am I now trying to win the approval of men, or of God? Or am I trying to please men? If I were still trying to please men, I would not be a servant of Christ." (Galatians 1:10)

STEPS TO SOLUTION

Life is full of confrontations—from birth to death. Parents confront the misbehavior of their children, couples confront the problematic behavior of their spouses, peers confront the unacceptable behavior of friends, employers confront the unsatisfactory behavior of employees, law enforcement officers confront the illegal behavior of citizens, and God confronts the sinful behavior of everyone.

Confrontation is inevitable and impossible to escape. Therefore, the question is not, "*Will* confrontation occur?" but "*How* will it occur?" How will *you* choose to confront troublesome behavior in your own life, and how will you confront it in the lives of others? Will you let emotion—fear, anger, frustration—dictate your actions? Or will you let God rule over your emotions and allow Him to direct your actions? If the Spirit of God indwells you, then you have everything you need to confront assertively. As you study and learn His ways of confronting, He will enable you to put His ways into practice.

"His divine power has given us everything we need for life and godliness through our knowledge of him who called us by his own glory and goodness."
(2 Peter 1:3)

Key Passage to Read

Matthew 18:15–17

Spiritual Steps for Confronting Offenders

▶ **Step One:** Confront Alone. (v. 15)

"If your brother sins against you, go and show him his fault, just between the two of you. If he listens to you, you have won your brother over."

- To preserve the dignity of the other person

- To show your personal concern for the other person

- To give occasion for clarifying motives

- To offer opportunity for repentance

- To provide the possibility of complete reconciliation

▶ **Step Two:** Confront with Witnesses. (v. 16)

"But if he will not listen, take one or two others along, so that 'every matter may be established by the testimony of two or three witnesses.'"

- To show the seriousness of the offense

- To express that other people have concern

- To confirm and clarify the accusation

- To offer a second opportunity for repentance

- To provide accountability and hope for change

▶ **Step Three:** Confront before the Church Body. (v. 17)

"If he refuses to listen to them, tell it to the church; and if he refuses to listen even to the church, treat him as you would a pagan or a tax collector."

- To reveal the severity of the offense
- To demonstrate proper confrontation to the entire church body
- To provide yet another opportunity for repentance
- To offer restoration of the person to the entire church body
- To discipline the unrepentant person for the sake of Christian unity

KEY VERSE TO MEMORIZE

"Brothers, if someone is caught in a sin, you who are spiritual should restore him gently. But watch yourself, or you also may be tempted. Carry each other's burdens, and in this way you will fulfill the law of Christ."
(Galatians 6:1–2)

Confront your sin and accept God's mercy.

You will never be ready and fully able to confront someone else until you've taken a confronting look at yourself from the inside out. You, like everyone else, were created to have a personal relationship with God, but sin has caused that relationship to be broken. There is only one way to a restored relationship with God—through His Son, Jesus. In order to be in right standing with God, you must confront the fact that you have sinned and you need God's mercy, His free gift that He is graciously offering to you through Jesus.

Receive God's Free Gift to You

The first step toward having a good relationship with God is understanding four important points from God's Word.

#1 **God's Purpose for You is *Salvation*.**

What was God's motive in sending Christ to earth?

To condemn you? No, to express His love for you by saving you!

"God so loved the world, that he gave his only Son, that whoever believes in him should not perish but have eternal life. For God did not send his Son into the world to condemn the world, but to save the world through him." (John 3:16–17)

What was Jesus' purpose in coming to earth?

To make everything perfect and to remove all sin? No, to forgive your sins, empower you to have victory over sin, and enable you to live a fulfilled life!

"I [Jesus] have come that they may have life, and have it to the full." (John 10:10)

#2 Your Problem is *Sin*.

What exactly is sin?

Sin is living *independently* of God's standard—knowing what is right, but choosing wrong.

"Anyone, then, who knows the good he ought to do and doesn't do it, sins." (James 4:17)

What is the major consequence of sin?

Spiritual death, spiritual separation from God.

"The wages of sin is death, but the gift of God is eternal life in Christ Jesus our Lord." (Romans 6:23)

#3 God's Provision for You is the *Savior*.

Can anything remove the penalty for sin?

Yes. Jesus died on the cross to personally pay the penalty for your sins.

"God demonstrates his own love for us in this: While we were still sinners, Christ died for us." (Romans 5:8)

What is the solution to being separated from God?

Belief in Jesus Christ as the only way to God the Father.

"Jesus answered, 'I am the way and the truth and the life. No one comes to the Father except through me.'" (John 14:6)

#4 Your Part is *Surrender.*

Place your faith in (rely on) Jesus Christ as your personal Lord and Savior and reject your "good works" as a means of gaining God's approval.

"It is by grace you have been saved, through faith—and this not from yourselves, it is the gift of God—not by works, so that no one can boast." (Ephesians 2:8–9)

Give Christ control of your life, entrusting yourself to Him.

"Jesus said to his disciples, 'If anyone would come after me, he must deny himself and take up his cross and follow me. For whoever wants to save his life will lose it, but whoever loses his life for me will find it. What good will it be for a man if he gains the whole world, yet forfeits his soul? Or what can a man give in exchange for his soul?'" (Matthew 16:24–26)

The moment you choose to believe in Him— entrusting your life to Christ—He gives you His Spirit to live inside you. Then the Spirit of Christ gives you His wisdom to make the right confrontations, and He enables you to live the fulfilled life God has planned for you. If you want to be fully forgiven by God and become the person God created you to be, you can tell Him in a simple, heartfelt prayer like this:

PRAYER OF SALVATION

*"God, I want a real relationship with You.
I admit that many times I've chosen to go
my own way instead of Your way.
Please forgive me for my sins.
Jesus, thank You for dying on the cross
to pay the penalty for my sins.
Come into my life to be
my Lord and my Savior.
Change me from the inside out and make me
the person You created me to be.
In Your holy name I pray. Amen."*

What Can You Expect Now?

If you sincerely prayed this prayer, you can know, as James did, that God will always give you His wisdom in every difficult situation you face!

**"If any of you lacks wisdom, he should ask God, who gives generously to all without finding fault, and it will be given to him."
(James 1:5)**

Self–evaluation Checklist[13]

☐ **Is your heart right?**[14]

- Look at the conflict from the offender's perspective. Listen in order to gain insight into thoughts, feelings, and concerns.

- Acknowledge that you are fallible. A good principle is: "When you are wrong, admit it. When you are right, don't say anything."[15]

- Take responsibility for your emotional reactions. You cannot blame someone else for your own emotional outbursts.

- Be humble. Is there something God is trying to teach you in this circumstance beyond the immediate conflict?

"Search me, O God, and know my heart; test me and know my anxious thoughts. See if there is any offensive way in me, and lead me in the way everlasting." (Psalm 139:23–24)

☐ **Is your tongue under control?** You may not realize that you have been offended until you are tempted to hurt someone with words. If you find yourself being sarcastic, giving subtle hints or jabs, talking behind someone's back, tearing down someone's reputation, lying, grumbling, or complaining, you are not in a position to confront in a loving way.[16]

"The good man brings good things out of the good stored up in his heart, and the evil man brings evil things out of the evil stored up in his heart. For out of the overflow of his heart his mouth speaks." (Luke 6:45)

☐ **Are you willing to ask forgiveness of your offender?** When you ask forgiveness for your own failures, often others are able to see and feel convicted of their own failure and will respond with, "Yes, and would you also forgive me?"[17]

"Confess your sins to each other." (James 5:16)

☐ **Have you forgiven your offender?** Forgiveness does not mean that you feel good about the person or the offense. Rather, it is the act of releasing that person from obligation to you. Forgiveness goes beyond justice—it is what God did for you when He accepted Christ's death in your place! You can forgive someone who offends you even if they never know they offended you.

"Bear with each other and forgive whatever grievances you may have against one another. Forgive as the Lord forgave you." (Colossians 3:13)

☐ **Have you prayed for your offender?** Pray for God to intervene and help the offender recognize sinful behavior and turn from it so that God will be glorified in the person's life.

"Far be it from me that I should sin against the LORD by failing to pray for you. And I will teach you the way that is good and right." (1 Samuel 12:23)

☐ **Do you care about your offender?** Make sure you approach the person you are seeking to correct with a prayerful and tender heart. A good sign that you really care about the person is that you find confronting difficult—this can show that you have thought through the issue from the offender's perspective.[18]

"Administer true justice; show mercy and compassion to one another." (Zechariah 7:9)

☐ **Are you sensitive to the pain of your offender?** There is an adage that says, "Hurt people hurt people."[19] Don't make your pain the central issue of a confrontation.

"Mourn with those who mourn." (Romans 12:15)

☐ **Does your goal for the confrontation match the level of offense?** You might be tempted to exaggerate the offense because you have not found comfort for your hurt. The severity of the encounter must be balanced to match the severity of the offense.

"He has showed you, O man, what is good. And what does the LORD require of you? To act justly and to love mercy and to walk humbly with your God." (Micah 6:8)

☐ **Will you complete the task and help your offender?** Are you willing to do what it takes to work with the offender to overcome sin patterns for the sake of your relationship and in obedience to God? Before you confront, make sure you are willing to invest the time and energy necessary to encourage the offender to overcome the offensive behavior.

"The punishment inflicted on him by the majority is sufficient for him. Now instead, you ought to forgive and comfort him, so that he will not be overwhelmed by excessive sorrow. ... Reaffirm your love for him." (2 Corinthians 2:6–8)

QUESTION: "Is it gossip or slander to ask someone for counsel about how to confront someone who has offended me?"

ANSWER: The principle of first confronting a person alone does not mean that you should not seek godly counsel about how to confront. While you should be careful with whom you talk, you may need to get advice before a difficult confrontation. The first step of actual confronting should be done privately because it is usually easier for the offender to accept what you are saying when you go alone.

> **"Listen to advice and accept instruction, and in the end you will be wise." (Proverbs 19:20)**

THE THREE Approaches for Confrontation[20]

After you decide that you are going to confront, you must decide the best way to confront so that the person can receive the maximum benefit. Since different methods produce different results, consider the following scenarios and how you can best use them to help the one you are confronting.

The apostle Paul used both face-to-face and written confrontation in his ministry to the early churches. His example of assertive confrontation through these two approaches is seen throughout His epistles and can be of great value to you as you seek to confront others in a godly way.

"Even when we were with you, we gave you this rule: 'If a man will not work, he shall not eat.' We hear that some among you are idle. They are not busy; they are busybodies. Such people we command and urge in the Lord Jesus Christ to settle down and earn the bread they eat." (2 Thessalonians 3:10–12)

Face-to-Face (generally the first choice)

ADVANTAGES

▶ Most personal form of communication

▶ Allows you visually to ...

  ▪ express your concern in person.

  ▪ see immediate reaction.

  ▪ read body language.

  ▪ hear tone of voice.

  ▪ receive immediate feedback.

  ▪ clarify misunderstanding.

  ▪ determine the acceptance or rejection of the confrontation.

▶ Allows the offender to visually see your concern and care through your facial expressions, eyes, and body language

DISADVANTAGES

▶ Most threatening to the offender and to the confronter

▶ Gives little time for offender to ponder your words and to process before responding

▶ Can be more emotional

▶ Offers less control over what is heard and what is said—may lead to regrettable statements

▶ Not preferable if you have engaged in a sexually immoral relationship with the one you are confronting

Telephone (generally the second choice)

ADVANTAGES

▶ Less formal than face-to-face

▶ Usually easier to set up the meeting

▶ Allows you direct confrontation with less intensity

▶ Sometimes provides more privacy than trying to meet in person

▶ Allows you to ...

  ▪ hear the immediate reaction.

  ▪ hear tone of voice.

  ▪ receive immediate feedback.

  ▪ clarify misunderstandings.

  ▪ determine the acceptance or rejection of the confrontation.

▶ Provides safety by allowing both parties the option of terminating the conversation

▶ Provides a better opportunity for repeated contact and follow-up

DISADVANTAGES

▶ Immediacy perhaps more threatening to the offender

▶ Gives the offender little time to process before reacting

▶ Doesn't allow you to express warmth or concern through your body language

▶ Can be more easily terminated by the offender before the conflict is resolved

Written (generally the third choice)

ADVANTAGES

▶ Offers the most objective scenario because it is not done in haste

▶ Provides control of wording, timing, expression

▶ Provides a healthy distance from a physical, sexual, or emotional abuser

▶ Allows for repeated reading of the letter for better understanding

▶ Sometimes makes your feelings known without your need to confront

DISADVANTAGES

▶ Such an established permanent record cannot be rescinded

- ▶ Certain negative behaviors need a more personal confrontation in order to address the need for change

- ▶ Offender can choose not to respond

- ▶ Follow-up conversation may be necessary to resolve conflict and pursue mutual forgiveness

- ▶ Copies of any written correspondence can be sent to others who are not involved in the difficult relationship

HOW TO Use the Sandwich Technique

When confronting someone who needs to be corrected, the "Sandwich Technique" has proved to be an effective way to both instruct and encourage at the same time. We all know how it feels to be unsuccessful, to have plans fail for lack of preparation, information, or skills—or to have relationships fail for lack of insight, discernment, or communication. We also know how it feels to fail because of blatant wrongdoing on our part, reacting angrily when disappointed, forcing compliance when pressured, or seeking retaliation when rejected. In such times, we need someone to come alongside us and, in a gentle, nonthreatening way, "set us straight" before we do even more harm.

"Brothers, if someone is caught in a sin, you who are spiritual should restore him gently." (Galatians 6:1)

The Sandwich Technique

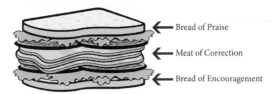

← Bread of Praise

← Meat of Correction

← Bread of Encouragement

▶ ***Bread of praise:*** Begin with a positive statement, a sincere compliment, or a genuine statement of loving care. Accentuate the positive aspect of the situation.

EXAMPLE: "I know this is a very difficult time for you, but I know you have the God-given courage and the ability to rise above this situation and turn it around. I would love to help you if you will let me."

"A man finds joy in giving an apt reply—and how good is a timely word!" (Proverbs 15:23)

▶ ***Meat of correction:*** Clarify the desired goal. Objectively recount the chain of events that led up to the present problem, examining what might have gone wrong and why. Problem-solve by brainstorming about possible options presently available for correcting the situation. Then determine a future course of action.

EXAMPLE: "Let's look at the situation and ask God to help us figure out what happened and how we can work on establishing a new strategy that will set you on a correction course and improve your chances of being successful."

"Whoever loves discipline loves knowledge, but he who hates correction is stupid." (Proverbs 12:1)

▶ *Bread of encouragement*: Conclude with a statement expressing confidence and assurance of future success.

EXAMPLE: "I've seen you overcome difficulties in the past, and I know you can do this. I'm extremely proud of you. I believe in you, and I believe in God, who lives within you. If you follow His leading and rely on Him for your sufficiency, you will succeed at everything He calls you to do."

"Encourage one another and build each other up, just as in fact you are doing." (1 Thessalonians 5:11)

CONDUCTING A One-on-One Confrontation

Set Your Goals for Confrontation

▶ *Don't* choose any setting where interruptions or distractions could easily occur. Suggest a place. "Let's meet in the conference room where we can have privacy and not be interrupted."

Do control the time and place as much as possible to minimize distractions and to maximize privacy and focus. A neutral setting is best where there are no telephone interruptions, television, music, or Internet distractions.

"There is a time for everything, and a season for every activity under heaven." (Ecclesiastes 3:1)

▶ ***Don't*** **become angry or defensive** at the negative reaction of those confronted. Avoid a statement like this: "Don't get mad at me. You're the one in the wrong!"

Do speak directly and honestly, but also gently and respectfully, knowing that the one you are speaking to needs a changed heart. "I realize this is difficult to hear, but we can work it out and get things resolved between us."

"A man of knowledge uses words with restraint, and a man of understanding is even-tempered." (Proverbs 17:27)

▶ ***Don't*** **speak for others.** "Some people feel like you ... "

Do keep the conversation personal! "I have noticed ... "

"The wise in heart are called discerning, and pleasant words promote instruction." (Proverbs 16:21)

▶ ***Don't*** **attack character.** "You're lazy, dishonest, greedy, hateful, irresponsible!"

Do address behavior—specific problematic patterns. "I'm concerned that you're not following through on your commitments. You're consistently late (getting your homework done, getting to work, getting to meetings)."

"Reckless words pierce like a sword, but the tongue of the wise brings healing." (Proverbs 12:18)

▶ ***Don't* use generalities or inference.** "You just need to change!"

Do speak in concrete, specific terms. "I'm concerned about the direction your life is going. When I (heard, saw) (action, behavior), I felt (sad, disappointed) because (state the reason)."

"The teaching of the wise is a fountain of life, turning a man from the snares of death." (Proverbs 13:14)

▶ ***Don't* use shaming tactics.** "Remember when you (failed, forgot, were caught)? You should feel horrible."

Do help the offender process any guilt or shame. "I know you must feel bad about your actions, and I do too. But God doesn't want you to be guilt-ridden, and neither do I. Can we talk about it and turn it over to Him?"

"Be kind and compassionate to one another, forgiving each other, just as in Christ God forgave you." (Ephesians 4:32)

▶ ***Don't* focus on your own pain.** "I continue to feel angry, hurt, frustrated."

Do focus on the offender's need to repent and change.

"He [the Lord] is patient with you, not wanting anyone to perish, but everyone to come to repentance." (2 Peter 3:9)

▶ ***Don't* shut off conversation or objectivity.** "I don't want to hear anything you have to say."

Do listen to the offender and be prepared to change your perspective of the offense.

"The heart of the righteous weighs its answers, but the mouth of the wicked gushes evil." (Proverbs 15:28)

▶ *Don't* **say, "You're hopeless" or act as though no hope exists.**

Do offer hope. Realize there are no hopeless people—only those who feel hopeless. God offers hope to everyone.

"'I know the plans I have for you,' declares the LORD, 'plans to prosper you and not to harm you, plans to give you hope and a future.'" (Jeremiah 29:11)

▶ *Don't* **put people "in cement," assuming they will never change.** "You'll never change! You'll always ... "

Do be patient, praying that as you plant seeds of truth, in time the person will change. Realize that people don't change overnight.

"Be patient with everyone." (1 Thessalonians 5:14)

▶ *Don't* **assume that a confrontation is wasted just because it ends in anger or rejection.** "I guess this was just a waste of time and energy."

Do be prepared for hostility and lack of cooperation. Some people need time to process a confrontation before they can take responsibility. Leave open an opportunity for further communication.

"The Lord's servant must not quarrel; instead, he must be kind to everyone. ... Those who oppose him he must gently instruct, in the hope that God will grant them repentance leading them to a knowledge of the truth, and that they will come to their senses and escape from the trap of the devil, who has taken them captive to do his will." (2 Timothy 2:24–26)

COMMON QUESTIONS about Confrontation

QUESTION: "How do I respond to someone who reacts defensively or with anger when confronted?"

ANSWER: You cannot control the response of others. If you lovingly and responsibly confront, yet people fail to respond appropriately, you may need to let them go by releasing them to God. Each person is directly accountable before God for their wrong behavior, and ultimately He will judge them justly.

"Each of us will give an account of himself to God." (Romans 14:12)

QUESTION: "If I have confronted someone for wrong behavior and that person continues to rebuff my words, should I continue to bring it up?"

ANSWER: If no change occurs after repeated attempts to confront someone who is clearly wrong, don't continue confronting. The Bible says,

"If anyone will not welcome you or listen to your words, shake the dust off your feet when you leave that home or town." (Matthew 10:14)

QUESTION: "If someone refuses to take responsibility when confronted, can I take that person to court? What can I legally do when someone has wronged me in a way that costs me materially or psychologically?"

ANSWER: The goal of confrontation is to correct someone who is at fault in order to ultimately bring unity and peace. Litigation is used when rights have been violated and a person refuses to accept responsibility. Litigation rarely results in unity or peace. That is why Scripture instructs Christians to settle their conflicts outside of court (1 Corinthians 6:1–7). Some disputes can best be settled with the help of others who will listen to both parties and then mediate a settlement (Matthew 18:15–17). With an unbeliever, although civil action is not forbidden, God's heart is still for reconciliation.

"As you are going with your adversary to the magistrate, try hard to be reconciled to him on the way, or he may drag you off to the judge, and the judge turn you over to the officer, and the officer throw you into prison." (Luke 12:58)

The Difference between Destructive and Constructive Confrontation

Destructive Confrontation

▶ Focuses on character

▶ Uses degrading, accusing, or threatening words to motivate change

▶ Assumes a negative motive in offensive behavior

▶ Gives no opportunity for apology or restitution

▶ Demands immediate correction as a condition for continued fellowship

▶ Imposes no consequences or disproportionate consequences

▶ Puts total responsibility for correction on the offender

Constructive Confrontation

▶ Focuses on behavior

▶ Uses loving, hopeful, and encouraging words to motivate change

▶ Assumes a desire to grow and become more like Christ

▶ Invites confession and is eager to forgive and seek reconciliation

▶ Allows for time to grow and learn better behaviors

▶ Offers appropriate consequences that develop character and responsibility

▶ Accepts responsibility for accountability through the change process

"Love is patient, love is kind. It does not envy, it does not boast, it is not proud. It is not rude, it is not self-seeking, it is not easily angered, it keeps no record of wrongs. Love does not delight in evil but rejoices with the truth. It always protects, always trusts, always hopes, always perseveres. Love never fails." (1 Corinthians 13:4–8)

MASTERING THE Assertive Style

The secret to mastering confrontation is to learn not only how to confront assertively, but also how to interact effectively with the different ways people respond. For example, your approach toward a passive person should be different from your approach toward an aggressive person.

The Key Components of Assertive Confrontation

▶ **Begin with a positive statement—a sincere compliment.**

- "I value our relationship. I appreciate your (name good character traits)."

▶ **Describe the unacceptable behavior and how it made you feel.** (Address only the facts. Make no personal attacks.)

- "The last three times that we agreed to leave at 8:45, you arrived late, and we didn't leave until after 9:00. Truthfully, being late makes me feel not only bad but also disrespected."

▶ **Present expectations.**

- "I would like for us to go together, but no matter what you choose to do, I have decided to be on time from this point forward."

▶ **Communicate consequences with a plan of accountability.**

- "In order to be on time next week, we need to leave by 8:45. If you're not here by then, I will have to leave without you. However, I'm hoping we can leave together."

"Instruct a wise man and he will be wiser still; teach a righteous man and he will add to his learning." (Proverbs 9:9)

1 Confronting "Avoiders"—The Assertive Approach to Passive People

Deal gently, but firmly with passive people. Fear of failure causes them to not want to take responsibility. Your goal as an assertive confronter is not to push passive people out of their comfort zone, but to elicit their cooperation and to get an agreed upon plan with accountability for a change of behavior. (Realize that acting assertively may feel aggressive to those who are passive.) Consider this example of confrontation with a passive person who is repetitively late.

▶ **Involve them in the problem and offer solutions. Counter their objections with encouragement that a change of behavior is possible.**

- "How do you feel about being late?" (Wait for a response.) "I'm glad to hear that you don't want to be late. What are you doing before coming here that causes you to be late? What creative alternative do you think would bring about a solution? What do you think about planning to be here at 8:30 instead of at 8:45? You could set your clock ahead fifteen minutes to help you to be on time."

▶ **Declare in specific, measurable terms what is to be expected.**

- "If we are to go together, I need you to be here by 8:45. I expect you to call me by 8:30 if you see that you cannot make it so that I can make other arrangements."

▶ **Give them simple choices to help them make decisions.**

- "Would you rather be here at 8:45 so that we can go together, or would you like for me to make other arrangements?"

▶ **Obtain their agreement to follow through, and hold them accountable.**

- "Are we in agreement that you will be here no later than 8:45?" (Wait for a response.) "Thank you! That means a lot to me. To make sure we're on the same track, will you call me at 8:30 to assure me that you are leaving on time? I feel sure you're not trying to be late and that in your heart you really do want to be on time."

**"Let the wise listen
and add to their learning,
and let the discerning get guidance."
(Proverbs 1:5)**

2 Confronting "Attackers"—The Assertive Approach to Aggressive People

Deal directly with those who are aggressive because they respond well to those who stand up to them. Consciously choose to be calm, yet bold. Determine that you will not be intimidated by fear or provoked to anger. The goal is not to win an argument, but to gain agreement that a change of behavior is necessary and then to devise a plan for change.

▶ **Reclaim whatever control of your life that you should not have given away.**

- "Until now, I have not said anything about your being late. However, being on time is an important value to me. In the future I plan to be on time even if it means going by myself; therefore, if we are going to go together, you need to be on time."

▶ **Give the aggressive person time to talk. Then say back what you heard.**

- "What I'm hearing you say is _____. Is that right? Is there anything else you want to say about that?"

▶ **Openly defuse a competitive atmosphere.**

- "I realize we don't see eye-to-eye on this subject. My expectation—wanting to be on time—is not a personal attack against you. To me, repetitive lateness is an issue of integrity—a destructive habit that only you have the power to change. Do you understand why this is important not just to me, but to you as well?" (Wait for a response.) "Good!"

▶ **Draw the line in the sand: State the principle and maintain it.**

- "I need you to make a commitment to be on time. If you won't make this a priority, I will make other arrangements to go by myself. You may not see this as an issue of integrity, but I do. Integrity involves being reliable and faithful to keep your word. Because I know you want to be a person of integrity, you need to develop the habit of being on time."

**"The man of integrity walks securely."
(Proverbs 10:9)**

3 Confronting "Ambushers"—The Assertive Response to Passive-Aggressive People

Deal directly and transparently with passive-aggressive people. Because they are afraid to state their desires through direct interaction, your goal is to confront their indirect attacks and motivate them to be open and direct with you.

▶ **Expose their offensive behavior while holding them accountable for the truth.**

- "You've been over 30 minutes late the last three times. Do you agree that this is true?"

▶ **Confront their covert issues with you by inviting direct and open criticism.**

- "Have I done something to offend you? Have I done something to cause you to be afraid of me? Is there a reason why you want to be late? Have you considered that it might be intentional?"

▶ **Hold them accountable to ask for what they want.**

- "I want you to talk with me directly and state explicitly what you want—I need that. I can't read your mind. Will you do that for me and, more importantly, for yourself?"

▶ **State your expectation of having direct communication between the two of you, along with the consequences of not doing so.**

- "I see that the underlying problem is not your lateness, but instead a lack of direct communication between the two of us. I realize that being late may not be an issue of integrity for you, but it is an issue of integrity to me. In the future, I will need you to be on time if we are to go together. Otherwise, we will go separately. But more importantly, I am expecting you to come to me about any problems you have with me. Can we agree on that?"

"The integrity of the upright guides them, but the unfaithful are destroyed by their duplicity." (Proverbs 11:3)

CRISIS CONFRONTATION for Chronic Problems[21]

What can you do when you confront a loved one who has a chronic problem—an addiction, a bad habit, or another behavior that is self-destructive or dangerous to others—and they refuse to change? When a personal confrontation is ineffective at bringing correction and life change, introduce the group dynamic—*there is power in numbers!*

Many times, personal confrontation and earnest appeals fall on deaf ears. Even when several individuals confront one-on-one, each plea is dismissed. As individuals, you are powerless—as a group, you are dynamite. A group can be empowered by God to move the immovable. God's Word lays out the blueprint for such an intervention.

> *"If your brother sins against you, go and show him his fault, just between the two of you. If he listens to you, you have won your brother over. But if he will not listen, take one or two others along, so that 'every matter may be established by the testimony of two or three witnesses.'"* (Matthew 18:15–16)

▶ Pray for wisdom and understanding from the Lord.

> *"The LORD gives wisdom, and from his mouth come knowledge and understanding."* (Proverbs 2:6)

▶ Educate yourself regarding the offender's particular addiction or besetting sin.

> *"The heart of the discerning acquires knowledge; the ears of the wise seek it out."* (Proverbs 18:15)

▶ Enlist the aid of the key people affected by the offender's harmful behavior—people who are willing to confront (caring family, friends, employer, coworkers, a spiritual leader).

> *"A truthful witness saves lives."* (Proverbs 14:25)

▶ In absolute confidentiality and without the offender present, hold a first meeting in which these key people rehearse what they will say, how they will say it, and the order in which they will speak when confronting.

"Better is open rebuke than hidden love. Wounds from a friend can be trusted." (Proverbs 27:5–6)

▶ Hold a second meeting with the offender present where one at a time each key confronter communicates genuine care for the offender and then shares the rehearsed confrontations—The Four *P*s of an Appeal.

"The tongue that brings healing is a tree of life, but a deceitful tongue crushes the spirit." (Proverbs 15:4)

The Four Ps of an Appeal[22]

#1 The Personal

▶ Affirm rather than attack.

- "I want you to know how much I value you (or love or care about you), and I am genuinely concerned about your behavior."

"Do not let any unwholesome talk come out of your mouths, but only what is helpful for building others up according to their needs, that it may benefit those who listen." (Ephesians 4:29)

#2 The Past

▶ Give a recent, specific example describing the offender's negative behavior and the personal impact it had on you.

- "Yesterday, when you were drunk and slurred your speech in front of my friend, I felt humiliated."

"A truthful witness gives honest testimony." (Proverbs 12:17)

- Be brief, keeping examples to three or four sentences.

"A man of knowledge uses words with restraint, and a man of understanding is even-tempered." (Proverbs 17:27)

#3 The Pain

▶ Emphasize the painful impact the addict's behavior has had on you by using "I" statements.

- "I felt deeply hurt and degraded because of the way you yelled at me."

"A wise man's heart guides his mouth, and his lips promote instruction." (Proverbs 16:23)

#4 The Plea

▶ Make a personal plea for your loved one to receive treatment.

- "I plead with you to get the help you need to overcome (_ offensive behavior _). If you are willing, you will have my help and deepest respect."

"The tongue has the power of life and death." (Proverbs 18:21)

▶ Be prepared to implement an immediate plan if treatment is agreed on.

- "Your bags have been packed, and you have been accepted into the treatment program at _____."

"Rescue those being led away to death; hold back those staggering toward slaughter. If you

say, 'But we knew nothing about this,' does not he who weighs the heart perceive it? Does not he who guards your life know it? Will he not repay each person according to what he has done?" (Proverbs 24:11–12)

▶ If treatment is refused, detail the repercussions.

- "We cannot allow you to come home or to be with our family until you have been clean and sober for (name a specific period of time)."

"Stern discipline awaits him who leaves the path; he who hates correction will die." (Proverbs 15:10)

WHAT IS the Best Response When You Are Confronted?[23]

"Whoever heeds correction is honored." (Proverbs 13:18)

▶ Make your relationship a priority over your personal rights.[24]

"The very fact that you have lawsuits among you means you have been completely defeated already. Why not rather be wronged? Why not rather be cheated?" (1 Corinthians 6:7)

▶ Demonstrate a heart willing to understand the other person's perspective. Be willing to change where necessary and to heal any relational tension.

"If it is possible, as far as it depends on you, live at peace with everyone." (Romans 12:18)

▶ Listen carefully even if you disagree with the other person's perspective. Give yourself time to consider what the other person says before you respond.

"Everyone should be quick to listen, slow to speak and slow to become angry." (James 1:19)

▶ Respond with humility. Give your reputation to God, and ask Him to help you with your relationships.

"Humble yourselves, therefore, under God's mighty hand, that he may lift you up in due time." (1 Peter 5:6)

▶ Consider those who confront you as being a gift from God. Flattery builds your pride, but confrontation helps you grow in the Lord.

"He who rebukes a man will in the end gain more favor than he who has a flattering tongue." (Proverbs 28:23)

▶ Maintain dignity and discernment. Allow God to speak to you through the other person. Your confronter may be someone who can help you get past an obstacle in your life. Even if you do not agree with your confronter, God may still use this opportunity for you to esteem the confronter for the courage displayed in confronting you and for the value placed on your relationship.

"He who ignores discipline despises himself, but whoever heeds correction gains understanding." (Proverbs 15:32)

▶ Do not be defensive or reactive, but consider the counsel of your confronter. God may be using that person to help you grow closer to Him. The benefits of confrontation may include coming closer to God, living a more loving lifestyle, and growing more intimate with your confronter.

"A man who remains stiff-necked after many rebukes will suddenly be destroyed—without remedy." (Proverbs 29:1)

THE FOUR Confrontation Styles Illustrated in the Gospels

The four Gospels shine a spotlight on the four different *styles* of confrontation, as seen just prior to the crucifixion of Christ. We can see each style highlighted because of memorable individuals who have shaped the course of human history.

▶ The Passive Avoider: Pontius Pilate

Pilate was a peace-at-any-price person. This Roman governor was faced with a difficult dilemma: What should he do with Jesus? Condemn Him or free Him? His personal fear of losing his powerful position—if mounting public unrest erupted into violence—was being pitted against the fate of an innocent man. He affirmed Jesus' innocence, but in the end he was too afraid to free Him from the snares of death. Rather than asserting himself, Pilate tried to quickly end his conflict by passing Jesus off to Herod. When that didn't work, he handed Jesus over to an angry mob, literally washing his hands of the matter.

"When Pilate saw that he was getting nowhere, but that instead an uproar was starting, he took water and washed his hands in front of the crowd. 'I am innocent of this man's blood,' he said. 'It is your responsibility!'" (Matthew 27:24)

▶ **The Aggressive Attackers: The Self-Righteous Pharisees**

Envious and exasperated, Israel's religious leaders incited the crowd into a murderous frenzy. Capitalizing on Pilate's character flaws, they coerced him into surrendering Jesus for crucifixion. This "brood of vipers" tested, tempted, and taunted Jesus at every turn, attacking him openly. They remained completely unwilling to embrace His teachings or the possibility that His claims might be true. In doing so, they not only missed their Messiah, but used Rome to crucify Him.

"The chief priests and the elders persuaded the crowd to ask for Barabbas and to have Jesus executed. ...'What shall I do, then, with Jesus who is called Christ?' Pilate asked. They all answered, 'Crucify him!' ... Then he released Barabbas to them. But he had Jesus flogged, and handed him over to be crucified." (Matthew 27:20, 22, 26)

▶ **The Passive-Aggressive Ambusher: Judas Iscariot**

For three years, Judas masqueraded as a devoted disciple ... cloaking dark motives with his privileged position. His protests against Mary's "wasting" expensive perfume to anoint Jesus' feet—funds better spent on the poor—were a decoy to disguise his own greed. Deceptive and covert, in a secret meeting with his conspirators, he accepted 30 pieces of silver in exchange for betraying Jesus. Even when it was time to identify Jesus to his enemies, this **ultimate ambusher** remained covert—going under the cover of darkness and sealing the Lord's fate with a kiss.

"The betrayer had arranged a signal with them: 'The one I kiss is the man; arrest him.' … But Jesus asked him, 'Judas, are you betraying the Son of Man with a kiss?'" (Matthew 26:48; Luke 22:48)

▶ The Assertive Activator: Jesus Christ

The Savior came that we *"may have life, and that [we] may have it more abundantly"* (John 10:10 NKJV). No motive has been more pure, no action more unselfish. His mission led him to confront evil at every turn—dishonest money changers, hypocritical religious leaders, corrupt government officials, common sinners. With each encounter, Jesus remains the only person in history who *always* assertively confronted sin with total integrity, flawless discernment, and perfectly chosen words.

"'I have spoken openly to the world,' Jesus replied. 'I always taught in synagogues or at the temple, where all the Jews come together. I said nothing in secret. Why question me? Ask those who heard me. Surely they know what I said.' When Jesus said this, one of the officials nearby struck him in the face. 'Is this the way you answer the high priest?' he demanded. 'If I said something wrong,' Jesus replied, 'testify as to what is wrong. But if I spoke the truth, why did you strike me?'" (John 18:20–23)

*The artist uses the hammer
and the chisel to remove bits of granite
in order to produce a beautiful sculpture.
God, the Master Sculptor, wants to take you
in His hands to use you as His hammer
and chisel to produce an extraordinary work
of art—Christlike character
in the one you confront.*

—June Hunt

SCRIPTURES TO MEMORIZE

Why are you to confront someone about **the error of his way**?

*"Remember this: Whoever turns a sinner from **the error of his way** will save him from death and cover over a multitude of sins."* (James 5:20)

In what way do **a fool** and **a wise man** differ?

*"The way of **a fool** seems right to him, but **a wise man** listens to advice."* (Proverbs 12:15)

What would help motivate me to **rebuke a wise man**?

*"Do not rebuke a mocker or he will hate you; **Rebuke a wise man** and he will love you."* (Proverbs 9:8)

Why should you **not lose heart when the Lord rebukes you**?

*"You have forgotten that word of encouragement that addresses you as sons: 'My son, Do not make light of the Lord's discipline, and **do not lose heart when he rebukes you**, because the Lord disciplines those he loves, and he punishes everyone he accepts as a son.'"* (Hebrews 12:5–6)

What should you do if someone **sins against you**?

*"If your brother **sins against you**, go and show him his fault, just between the two of you. If he listens to you, you have won your brother over."* (Matthew 18:15)

What will you **gain** if you **heed correction**?

> *"He who ignores discipline despises himself, but whoever **heeds correction gains** understanding."* (Proverbs 15:32)

Before you confront, what should you remove from "**your own eye**"?

> *"How can you say to your brother, 'Let me take the speck out of your eye,' when all the time there is a plank in your own eye? You hypocrite, first take the plank out of **your own eye**, and then you will see clearly to remove the speck from your brother's eye."* (Matthew 7:4–5)

Should you **trust a friend** who **wounds** you with the truth?

> *"**Wounds** from **a friend** can be **trusted**, but an enemy multiplies kisses."* (Proverbs 27:6)

How should I confront **someone caught in a sin**?

> *"Brothers, If **someone** is **caught in a sin**, you who are spiritual should restore him gently. But watch yourself, or you also may be tempted."* (Galatians 6:1)

What is the difference between the one who **ignores discipline** and the one who **heeds correction**?

> *"He who **ignores discipline** comes to poverty and shame, but whoever **heeds correction** is honored."* (Proverbs 13:18)

NOTES

1. Leslie Brown, ed., *The New Shorter Oxford English Dictionary on Historical Principles*, 2 vols., s.v. "confrontation" (Oxford: Clarendon, 1993), 477.

2. Richard Whitaker, *Whitaker's Revised BDB Hebrew-English Lexicon*, electronic edition, s.v. "tokhot" (Norfolk, VA: BibleWorks, 1995), BibleWorks v. 6.0.

3. Timothy Friberg and Barbara Friberg, *Analytical Lexicon to the Greek New Testament*, electronic ed., s.v. "parable" (Grand Rapids: Baker, 2000), BibleWorks v. 6.0.

4. W. E. Vine, Merrill F. Unger, and William White, *Vine's Complete Expository Dictionary of Old and New Testament Words*, electronic ed., s.v. "admonish" (Nashville: Thomas Nelson, 1996), Logos 2.1b.

5. Vine, *Vine's Complete Expository Dictionary*, s.v. "rebuke."

6. Vine, *Vine's Complete Expository Dictionary*, s.v. "rebuke."

7. John Nieder and Thomas M. Thompson, *Forgive & Love Again: Healing Wounded Relationships* (Eugene, OR: Harvest House, 1991), 151–55.

8. Deborah Smith Pegues, *Confronting Without Offending: Biblical Strategies for Effective Personal and Business Confrontation* (Tulsa, OK: Vincom, 1995), 3.

9. Nieder and Thompson, *Forgive & Love Again*, 156–60.

10. Josh McDowell, *Resolving Conflict* (Pomona, CA: Focus on the Family, 1989), 6–8; Ken Sande, *The Peacemaker: A Biblical Guide to Resolving Personal Conflict*, 3rd ed. (Grand Rapids: Baker, 2004), 22–29.

11. David Augsburger, *Caring Enough to Confront*, rev. ed. (Ventura, CA: Regal, 1981), 17–21; Pegues, *Confronting Without Offending*, 8–31.

12. Lawrence J. Crabb, Jr., *Understanding People: Deep Longings for Relationship*, Ministry Resources Library (Grand Rapids: Zondervan, 1987), 15–16; Robert S. McGee, *The Search for Significance*, 2nd ed. (Houston, TX: Rapha, 1990), 27–30.

13. Nieder and Thompson, *Forgive & Love Again*, 161–66.

14. McDowell, *Resolving Conflict*, 8–10.

15. McDowell, *Resolving Conflict*, 9.

16. Sande, *The Peacemaker*, 121–22; Pegues, *Confronting Without Offending*, 29.

17. Nieder and Thompson, *Forgive & Love Again*, 163.

18. Nieder and Thompson, *Forgive & Love Again*, 163.

19. Nieder and Thompson, *Forgive & Love Again*, 163.

20. Nieder and Thompson, *Forgive & Love Again*, 164–66.

21. Stephen Van Cleave, Walter Byrd, and Kathy Revell, *Counseling for Substance Abuse and Addiction*, edited by Gary R. Collins, Resources for Christian Counseling, vol. 12 (Dallas: Word, 1987), 83–86; Carolyn Johnson, *Understanding Alcoholism* (Grand Rapids: Zondervan, 1991), 145–50; Christina B. Parker, *When Someone You Love Drinks Too Much: A Christian Guide to Addiction, Codependence, & Recovery* (New York: Harper & Row, 1990), 55–56.

22. Van Cleave, Byrd, and Revell, *Counseling for Substance Abuse and Addiction*, 87.

23. Carole Mayhall, *Words That Hurt, Words That Heal* (Colorado Springs, CO: NavPress, 1986), 88–90.

24. Sande, *The Peacemaker*, 92–98.

June Hunt's HOPE FOR THE HEART minibooks are biblically-based, and full of practical advice that is relevant, spiritually-fulfilling and wholesome.

HOPE FOR THE HEART TITLES

www.hendricksonrose.com